THE ONLY
THING
HOTTER
THAN
MY FORGE
IS MY
WIFE

NAME

Made in the USA
Monee, IL
07 July 2026